KEYBOARDING

For Microcomputer, Word Processor & Typewriter

A SHORT COURSE

Willena Stanford

James Miller

David Bruce Miller

Longman Business Education
520 North Dearborn Street ·
Chicago, Illinois 60610-4975

© 1988 by Longman Group USA Inc.

Published in the United States of America by Longman Business Education, A Division of Longman Group USA Inc.

Adapted from *Keyboarding: A Short Course*, published by Copp Clark Pitman Ltd., Toronto, 1983.

Acquisitions Editor: Barbara Wood Donner
Project Editor: Marguerite Duffy
Copy Editor: Rita Tatum
Cover Designer: Stuart Paterson

ISBN: 0-88462-745-4

Printed in Canada. ·

88 89 90 10 9 8 7 6 5 4 3 2 1

Library of Congress Cataloging-in-Publication Data

Stanford, Willena.
   Keyboarding for microcomputer, word processor & typewriter.

   1. Typewriting.   2. Word processing.   3. Electronic data processing—Keyboarding.   I. Miller, James (James W.)   II. Miller, David Bruce.   III. Title.
Z49.S79 1988   652'.5   87-29736
ISBN 0-88462-745-4

ACKNOWLEDGMENTS

To the following people who reviewed and/or class-tested *Keyboarding for Microcomputer, Word Processor & Typewriter: A Short Course,* the authors and publisher would like to extend our sincere appreciation:

Harris Armstrong, Assistant Business Education Director, Cedarbrae Collegiate Institute

Evelyn Boyechko, Senior Typing Instructor, Success-Angus Business College

Michael East, Customer Support Representative, Radio Shack Computer Centre

Margaret Francis, Co-ordinator of Word Processing, Centennial College, Warden Woods Campus

Bob Peacock, Business Education Co-ordinator, Vancouver School Board

INTRODUCTION

Keyboarding for Microcomputer, Word Processor & Typewriter: A Short Course has been developed to teach students to input by touch on a computer keyboard. Because of the similarities between typewriter and computer keyboards either type of equipment can be used.

The ideal situation, of course, is to have the learners use computer equipment so that they can see their results on the video display unit above the keyboard. However, learners can simulate computer keyboards on their typewriter keyboards by depressing the shift lock key.

KEYBOARDING VS. TYPEWRITING

The skills of keyboarding and typewriting are very similar in that both require that learners be able to use keyboards quickly and accurately, know basic machine parts, use correct posture and technique, and be able to make decisions and handle applications. There are differences, however. A course in typewriting includes centering, tabulation, setting margins, line spacing, typing letters, memos, business forms, etc. A course in keyboarding does not include these topics because the computer can be programmed to set up (format) work. Commands to center and tabulate can be done after the information has been "input" or "entered" via the extra keys (coding keys) on a computer keyboard.

WHERE IS KEYBOARDING USED?

Keyboarding is used in many different jobs and locations. For example, airline reservations clerks use keyboarding to determine space and seat availability; office personnel use keyboarding to update records, send hundreds of letters yet enter the information only once, transmit information to branch locations; hospital workers use keyboarding for medical records and inventory control, etc. Students use keyboarding for such courses as information/word processing and computer programming. Many people keyboard on home computers. Because computers are becoming more common in the work and home environment, most people would benefit from a course in keyboarding.

SUGGESTED LEARNING PROGRAMS

Keyboarding for Microcomputer, Word Processor & Typewriter: A Short Course has been designed for use by keyboarders with varying levels of ability. It can be used by the person who has no knowledge of the keyboard, or by the typist in need of exposure to computer terminology and applications.

If it is a teacher-assisted class, the instructor and learner will choose the program which meets the learner's need. If *Keyboarding for Microcomputer, Word Processor & Typewriter: A Short Course* is being used as a self-study text, choose the program which best fits the individual's need, equipment being used, and time available. Of course the more time spent, the better your result.

I. **Six- to Eight-hour Introductory Program on a Computer Keyboard**
   Choose this program if the learner cannot keyboard and has limited time.
   A. Numbers, pages 1-3 *or* 4-6
   B. Alphabetic Keys, pages 12-26
   C. Correcting Errors, page 27
   D. Computer Words and Special Characters, pages 41-45
   E. Computer Applications, pages 48-57

II. **Twenty-five-hour Competency Program on a Computer Keyboard *or* a Typewriter Keyboard**
   Choose this program if the learner cannot keyboard and has time to complete the course.
   A. Numbers, pages 1-3 *or* 4-6
   B. All remaining pages in the text

III. **Twenty-five-hour Competency Program Beginning on a Typewriter Keyboard and Ending on a Computer Keyboard**
   Choose this program if the learner cannot keyboard and has time to complete the course.
   A. On the Typewriter Keyboard, complete pages 1-3, 12-26, and 29-40.
   B. On the Computer Keyboard, complete pages 4-11, 27, 29-32, and 41-57.

IV. **Three- to four-hour Refresher Program**
   Choose this brief program if the learner has taken at least one course in typewriting and wants to review previous learning, or become familiar with the computer keyboard.
   A. Numbers, pages 1-3 *or* 4-6
   B. Alphabetic Review, pages 29-33
   C. Corrections, page 27
   D. Computer Words and Special Characters, pages 41-45
   E. Computer Applications, pages 48-57

TO THE INSTRUCTOR AND INDIVIDUAL USER
ORGANIZATION OF THE TEXT

Keyboarding for Microcomputer, Word Processor & Typewriter: A Short Course is organized into ten components with the major stress on the numeric and alphabetic keyboards along with an introduction to special computer keyboard characters. The computer language BASIC has been used in parts of the text. It is important that keyboarders become familiar with BASIC command words and special characters. Because students of varying levels of expertise and ability will be using the text, all or some of the components may be used. Thus, a course in computer keyboarding could be as short as eight hours or as long as twenty-five hours. Keyboarding skills attained will vary based upon individual ability, motivation, and time available.

I. **Numeric Row Keys, pages 1-3**

The numbers are taught first because most computer languages begin each line with a line number. This component should be used by the student who will be using a computer keyboard that has the numbers on the fourth row of the keyboard. The numeric row keys are introduced by having the student move his/her hands directly to the fourth row. Numbers are easier to master if students are taught them from the fourth row. Also, if students later use a computer with a ten-key pad, he/she must remove his/her hands from the traditional alphabetic home row in order to input numeric information using the number pad.

II. **The Number Pad, pages 4-6**

This component introduces the learner to touch keyboarding of numbers. It is faster to keyboard numbers from a number pad than from the fourth row of the keyboard.

III. **Number Practice, pages 7-11**

This component may be used by all learners regardless of the previous method used to introduce the numbers. The exercises may be used immediately following the introduction of numbers and/or integrated with practice from the remaining parts of the text. It is probably wise for students to have three to five minutes of number practice each day that they are learning the alphabetic keyboard. The amount of time available to the individual learner will determine whether or not she/he will have an opportunity to do these exercises.

IV. **Alphabetic Keys, pages 12-26**

The alphabetic keys are introduced in the traditional manner. The number of times the learner enters each line will depend on the time available. However, the learner should have sufficient practice on this component so that he/she will be able to keyboard at a rate of 14 to 21 words per minute upon the completion of the section.

V. **Correcting Errors, pages 27-28**

Students should not take the time to correct errors while they are learning the alphabetic and numeric keys. The instructor will tell students when all lines must be keyboarded correctly. Such practice would probably begin during the Alphabetic Practice component.

VI. **Alphabetic Practice, pages 29-40**

This component will enable learners to consolidate skills in alphabetic keyboarding and permit them to work towards a keyboarding goal of 21 to 28 words a minute (GWPM). Unless learners have more than eight hours for keyboard learning and practice, this component may need to be omitted.

VII. **BASIC Computer Language Words, pages 41-42**

This component stresses the instructional words for BASIC computer language and should be practiced until the learner can keyboard the words at a rate of 4 to 5 lines per minute. If students will be using a computer language other than BASIC, the instructor should prepare a list of computer language words that will benefit the learners.

VIII. **Special Characters in BASIC, pages 43-45**

This component stresses the use of special characters in BASIC and should be practiced until the learner is familiar with their locations on the keyboard.

IX. Upper and Lower Case Letters, pages 46-47

This component is included for learners who will be working with computers that output in both upper and lower case letters. Consequently, it will not be necessary for all keyboarders to complete this section.

X. Computer Applications, pages 48-57

This component of 10 simple programs will introduce learners to the entering and running of programs. The keyboarder must keyboard all lines with 100 percent accuracy. If typewriter keyboards are used, there should be one computer with a large video display unit (television set) available so that the keyboarder may observe the programs being RUN. Time available will determine whether or not this section is completed.

SAMPLE LESSON— ALPHABETIC KEYS   T   Y

This lesson has been prepared for a 20-30 minute session.
First: Review practice from pages 17 and/or 16 (3-5 minutes).
Second: Number practice exercise/s from pages 7 to 11 (3-5 minutes).
Third: New lesson, letters T and Y, from page 18 (10-20 minutes).

Note: The cycle would be repeated two or three times in a one-hour time period depending upon the ability and motivation of the learner.

TO THE KEYBOARDER USING A TYPEWRITER

- Move the **paper guide** to the extreme left edge of the machine.
- Set the **left margin** 10 spaces in from the left edge of the machine.
- Set the **right margin** at the extreme right of the machine.
- Insert your paper into the machine.
- Space down 12 lines and insert your paper under the paper bail.
- Keep the **shift lock** depressed at all times unless you are entering numbers.
- Release the **shift lock** to enter numbers and certain special characters.
- Set the **line space indicator** for double spacing (DS).
- Enter the zero as 0, but notice that computers output the zero as 0̸.

PROPER POSTURE FOR KEYBOARDING

- Keep your eyes on the copy except when learning new reaches.
- Sit erect with feet flat on the floor. Place one foot slightly ahead of the other.
- Keep elbows and upper arms comfortably close to the body.

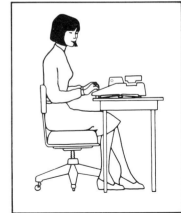

CONTENTS

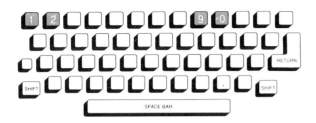

BEGIN ON PAGE 4 IF THE EQUIPMENT HAS A NUMBER PAD TO THE RIGHT OF THE ALPHABETIC KEYS.

FINGER POSITION

- Place the left index finger on the 4 key and let the remaining fingers fall into place on the 3, 2, and 1 keys.
- Place the right index finger on the 7 key and let the remaining fingers fall into place on the 8, 9, and 0 keys.
- These keys are known as the *numeric home row* keys.

INSTRUCTIONS

Enter each line twice.

The 2-digit number at the beginning of each line represents a *program line number* and is followed by a decimal and a space. The decimal is used after a line number when the data begins with a number. Otherwise the computer would respond to the line number as part of the data.

Note: Return your fingers to the numeric home row (4, 3, 2, 1 and 7, 8, 9, 0) after entering the decimal.

To get a space when required, tap the **space bar** with the thumb. (Be consistent in your choice of thumb.)

After entering the last number in the line, press the **return key**.

SPECIAL NOTE

You enter the zero in the same way that you enter other characters, i.e. by pressing the 0 key. However, computers output the zero as Ø.

```
1Ø.  111  ØØØ  111  ØØØ  111  ØØØ  111  ØØØ
1Ø.  1Ø1  1Ø1  1Ø1  1Ø1  Ø1Ø  Ø1Ø  Ø1Ø  Ø1Ø
11.  222  999  222  999  222  999  222  999
11.  292  292  292  292  929  929  929  929
12.  121  Ø9Ø  121  Ø9Ø  121  Ø9Ø  121  Ø2Ø
12.  212  9Ø9  212  9Ø9  212  9Ø9  212  9Ø9
19.  129  12Ø  29Ø  9Ø1  9Ø2  Ø12  Ø29  1Ø2
19.  1Ø9  2Ø1  2Ø2  2Ø9  9Ø1  9Ø2  9Ø2  Ø12
2Ø.  1Ø1  Ø1Ø  292  929  1Ø1  Ø1Ø  292  929
2Ø.  111  ØØØ  222  999  1Ø1  292  Ø1Ø  929
```

Numeric Row Keys   1 · 2 · 9 · 0 ————————————————————— 1

"Sales Bonus"

USING THE PROGRAM

There are 10 sales representatives in this exercise. The first one earned $10,500 during the year.

After you have RUN the program once, change the DATA lines.

Enter 5 new pieces of DATA on each of lines 130 and 140.

Now RUN the program again.

```
30   PRINT "NO."; TAB(10); "SALARY"; TAB(20);
     "BONUS"
40   LET T = 0
50   FOR L = 1 TO 10
60   READ S
70   LET B = (INT(S/12*100))/100
80   LET T = T + B
90   PRINT L; TAB(10); S; TAB(20); B
100  NEXT L
110  PRINT
120  PRINT "TOTAL BONUS $"; T
130  DATA 10500, 9850, 11500, 8840, 9000
140  DATA 7700, 15000, 14560, 25000, 19000
150  END
RUN
```

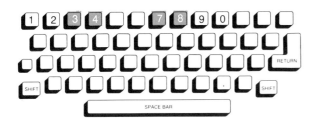

FINGER POSITION

- Place the left index finger on the 4 key and let the remaining fingers fall into place on the 3, 2, and 1 keys.
- Place the right index finger on the 7 key and let the remaining fingers fall into place on the 8, 9, and 0 keys.

INSTRUCTIONS

Enter each line twice.

Keep your eyes on the copy in the book.

Say each number to yourself as you enter it.

Do not be concerned with errors at this time.

1Ø.	111	ØØØ	222	999	1Ø1	Ø1Ø	292	929
11.	333	888	333	888	333	888	333	888
12.	383	383	383	383	838	838	838	838
13.	321	89Ø	321	89Ø	123	Ø98	123	Ø98
14.	444	777	444	777	444	777	444	777
2Ø.	474	474	474	474	747	747	747	747
21.	432	789	432	789	234	987	234	987
23.	347	348	349	34Ø	781	782	783	784
24.	378	389	39Ø	37Ø	812	823	834	814
27.	123	124	321	214	789	78Ø	798	79Ø
28.	213	214	218	219	217	219	21Ø	212
29.	781	782	783	784	789	78Ø	347	784
3Ø.	123	234	247	478	789	89Ø	321	432
31.	743	874	987	Ø98	784	783	782	781
32.	431	432	437	328	439	43Ø	239	8Ø7

"Smallest Number"

USING THE PROGRAM

After you have RUN the program once, change the < sign to > and in line 60 change "SMALLEST NUMBER IS" to "LARGEST NUMBER IS." Now RUN the program again.

These 2 small changes permit the computer to select the largest number out of the same given list.

```
15 READ N
20 FOR K = 1 TO N
25 READ R(K)
30 NEXT K
35 LET S = 1
40 FOR I = 2 TO N
45 IF R(S)<R(I) THEN 55
50 LET S = I
55 NEXT I
60 PRINT "SMALLEST NUMBER IS "; R(S)
65 DATA 9, 45, 43, 42, 44, 41
70 DATA 44, 48, 53, 49
75 END
RUN
```

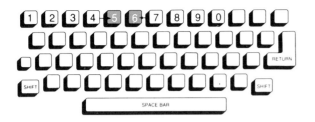

FINGER POSITION

- Place the left index finger on the 4 key and let the remaining fingers fall into place on the 3, 2, and 1 keys.
- Place the right index finger on the 7 key and let the remaining fingers fall into place on the 8, 9, and 0 keys.
- Use the 4 finger to enter the 5 key.
- Use the 7 finger to enter the 6 key.

INSTRUCTIONS

Enter each line twice.

Keep your eyes on the copy in the book.

If time permits, practice exercises from the Number Practice section, pages 7-11.

1Ø.	444	777	444	777	474	747	474	747
11.	454	767	454	767	454	767	454	767
12.	555	666	555	666	555	666	555	666
13.	454	767	545	676	454	767	545	676
14.	546	675	645	657	756	766	455	565
15.	41Ø	7Ø1	334	956	154	282	4Ø2	352
16.	7ØØ	515	931	236	Ø83	248	417	843
17.	858	237	695	193	676	822	9Ø4	197
18.	267	787	646	955	393	265	524	Ø18
19.	35Ø	116	573	939	864	736	572	418
2Ø.	ØØ8	323	534	126	438	335	53Ø	194
21.	548	827	784	371	156	186	7Ø3	737
22.	389	298	Ø48	741	768	82Ø	69Ø	262
23.	5Ø2	122	565	Ø2Ø	6Ø4	633	249	571
24.	816	478	686	932	3Ø8	617	1Ø6	13Ø

"Rolling a Die"

USING THE PROGRAM

In this particular exercise 1 die was rolled 1,000 times.

RUN the program a second, third, and fourth time. What do you notice about the results each time?

Be patient for the results after entering RUN. The computer must roll the die 1,000 times.

```
20   DIM X(6)
30   FOR I = 1 TO 6
40   LET X(I) = 0
50   NEXT I
60   FOR I = 1 TO 1000
70   LET R = INT(1+6*RND(1))
80   LET X(R) = X (R) + 1
90   NEXT I
100  PRINT "NO."; TAB(10); "TIMES"
110  FOR I = 1 TO 6
120  PRINT I; TAB(10); X(I)
130  NEXT I
140  END
RUN
```

Number Pad

BEGIN ON PAGE 1 IF THE EQUIPMENT HAS THE NUMBERS ON THE TOP ROW OF THE KEYBOARD.

FINGER POSITION

- Place the right index finger on the 4 key and let the next two fingers fall into place on the 5 and 6 keys. These keys are known as the numeric home row keys.
- Use the 6 finger to enter the decimal key.

INSTRUCTIONS

Enter each line twice.

The 2-digit number at the beginning of each line represents a program line number and is followed by a decimal and a space. The decimal is used after a line number when the data begins with a number. Otherwise the computer would respond to the line number as part of the data. *Note:* Some computers will automatically put the space in after the line number for you.

To get a space when required, tap the **space bar** with the right thumb.

After entering the last number in the line, press the **return key**.

SPECIAL NOTE

You enter the zero in the same way that you enter other characters i.e. by pressing the 0 key. However, computers output the zero as Ø.

44.	444	555	666	444	555	666	555	666
45.	454	464	454	464	454	464	454	464
46.	545	565	545	565	545	565	545	565
54.	646	656	646	656	646	656	646	656
55.	456	564	645	456	564	645	564	645
56.	465	546	654	465	546	654	546	654
64.	445	556	664	445	556	664	554	665
65.	455	566	644	455	566	644	556	445
66.	466	544	655	466	544	655	446	554

"Flipping a Coin"

INSTRUCTIONS

Enter your name on line 10.

Enter a program title on line 20.

USING THE PROGRAM

After you have RUN, the program once, enter the word LIST and then enter the word RUN. Are the second results the same as the first? *Note:* line 60 simulates the flipping of a coin using a computer generated random number.

RUN the program several times if you wish.

```
10   REM YOUR NAME
20   REM HEADS AND TAILS
30   LET H=0
40   LET T=0
50   FOR J = 1 TO 100
60   LET X = INT(2*RND(1))
70   IF X=1 THEN 110
80   PRINT "T";
90   LET T=T+1
100  GOTO 130
110  PRINT "H";
120  LET H=H+1
130  NEXT J
140  PRINT
150  PRINT "NUMBER OF HEADS "; H
160  PRINT "NUMBER OF TAILS "; T
170  END
RUN
```

Number Pad

FINGER POSITION

- Place the right index finger on the 4 key and let the next 2 fingers fall into place on the 5 and 6 keys.
- Use the 4 finger to enter the 1 key.
- Use the 5 finger to enter the 2 key.
- Use the 6 finger to enter the 3 key.
- Use the right thumb to enter the Ø key.

INSTRUCTIONS

Enter each line twice.

Keep your eyes on the copy in the book.

Say each number to yourself as you enter it.

Do not be concerned with errors at this time.

```
1Ø.  444 555 666 454 564 645 464 656
11.  455 566 644 554 665 446 544 655
12.  414 414 525 525 636 636 414 525
13.  636 414 525 636 141 252 363 4ØØ
14.  212 232 2Ø2 212 232 2Ø2 212 2Ø2
15.  313 323 3Ø3 313 323 3Ø3 323 3Ø3
16.  123 23Ø 3Ø1 Ø12 123 23Ø 3Ø1 Ø12
2Ø.  132 2Ø3 31Ø Ø21 132 2Ø3 31Ø Ø21
21.  112 223 33Ø ØØ1 322 11Ø 233 Ø11
22.  311 122 ØØ2 233 Ø22 331 11Ø 221
23.  221 332 ØØ3 1ØØ 211 322 112 Ø33
24.  141 415 526 243 634 351 162 534
25.  261 653 431 135 326 541 235 614
26.  114 225 336 ØØ4 155 Ø66 441 55Ø
3Ø.  662 2ØØ 455 366 511 422 633 ØØ4
```

INSTRUCTIONS

Line 10 gives the name of the student. You may use your own name instead.

Line 20 gives the name of the program.

USING THE PROGRAM

The first number 4000 in line 50 has the effect of instructing the computer to stop computing the batting averages.

The first, third, fifth etc. numbers in lines 40 and 50 are the number of "at bats" and the second, fourth, sixth etc. numbers are the "hits". Put your own DATA into lines 40 and 50 and RUN the program again.

Remember to make the first of the final 2 numbers 4000. A final number must be given, but its value is irrelevant.

```
10   REM DAVID HAGEN
20   REM BATTING AVERAGES
30   READ B,H
40   DATA 15, 5, 31, 12, 25, 4, 17, 7
50   DATA 36, 11, 24, 4, 45, 18, 4000, 4000
60   IF B=4000 THEN 100
70   LET A=(INT(H/B*1000))/1000
80   PRINT "AT BATS "; B; TAB(13); "HITS "; H;
     TAB(25); "AVG. "; A
90   GOTO 30
100  PRINT "END OF RUN"
110  END
RUN
```

Number Pad

FINGER POSITION

- Place the right index finger on the 4 key and let the next two fingers fall into place on the 5 and 6 keys.
- Use the 4 finger to enter the 7 key.
- Use the 5 finger to enter the 8 key.
- Use the 6 finger to enter the 9 key.

INSTRUCTIONS

Enter each line twice.

Keep your eyes on the copy in the book.

If time permits, practice exercises from the Number Practice section, pages 7-11.

37.	444	555	666	111	222	333	Ø00	456
38.	123	64Ø	551	112	33Ø	141	266	Ø32
39.	474	474	585	585	696	696	474	585
4Ø.	696	474	585	696	747	858	969	789
47.	414	474	525	585	636	696	1ØØ	7ØØ
48.	897	978	798	879	987	798	879	987
49.	778	889	997	778	889	997	788	899
5Ø.	977	788	899	977	887	998	779	887
57.	998	779	877	988	799	877	988	799
58.	771	772	773	77Ø	774	775	776	711
59.	722	733	7ØØ	744	755	766	177	188
6Ø.	199	1ØØ	122	133	144	155	166	117
67.	118	119	11Ø	112	113	114	115	116
68.	147	852	369	Ø57	7Ø4	689	286	5Ø1
69.	923	459	198	45Ø	231	762	951	48Ø

Each line in the BASIC computer language must begin with a number. The lines are usually numbered in increments of 5 or 10.

A number never precedes the words RUN and LIST in the BASIC computer language.

It is not necessary to leave any spaces on a computer keyboard. However, spaces between words and symbols make the lines easier to read and to check.

Notice that there is a space after the " so that there will be a space between words when they are printed.

INSTRUCTIONS

Enter the program on the right.

USING THE PROGRAM

In lines 50, 60, and 70 change each semicolon (;) to a comma (,) and RUN the program a second time.

Note: If you are using a typewriter keyboard, you will have to release the **shift key** before entering the semicolon, otherwise a colon will be entered.

```
10 LET A$= " ALL"
20 LET B$= " HUMANS"
30 LET C$= " ARE"
40 LET D$= " MORTALS"
50 PRINT A$; B$; C$; D$
60 PRINT A$; D$; C$; B$
70 PRINT B$; C$; A$; D$
80 END
RUN
```

Computer Applications

INSTRUCTIONS

Enter each line twice.

Keep your eyes on the copy in the book.

EXERCISE 1

1Ø. 174 161 985 963 477 472 533 934
15. 413 812 815 967 315 33Ø 85Ø 411
2Ø. Ø95 97Ø 627 368 161 9ØØ 87Ø 744
25. Ø84 778 275 Ø3Ø 667 134 355 888
3Ø. 476 45Ø 492 871 346 ØØ6 632 375

EXERCISE 2

35. 864 Ø18 279 943 789 814 Ø27 Ø46
4Ø. 129 685 872 488 47Ø 787 59Ø 454
45. 3Ø5 594 269 867 836 3Ø8 1Ø7 786
5Ø. 663 331 299 994 326 864 146 511
55. 325 421 188 898 762 999 327 335

EXERCISE 3

6Ø. 137 396 194 581 25Ø 546 Ø68 83Ø
65. 511 721 265 Ø63 ØØ3 8Ø7 539 535
7Ø. 756 685 912 6Ø5 654 336 497 Ø1Ø
75. 522 59Ø 661 88Ø 314 765 416 282
8Ø. 462 288 51Ø 381 429 Ø74 265 174

Number Practice _____ 7

INSTRUCTIONS

Enter the program on the right.

USING THE PROGRAM

After you have RUN the program, enter the word LIST and strike the **return key**.

Now enter the following line:

```
10 PRINT "MARY ANN PLAYS THE HARP."
```

Now enter the word LIST and press the **return key**. What do you see?

Now enter the word RUN and press the **return key**. What do you see?

Again, enter the word LIST and press the **return key**. Now enter the following line:

```
56 PRINT "EVERYONE ENJOYS VIOLINS."
```

Enter the word LIST on the next line and press the **return key**. What do you see?

Enter the word RUN and press the **return key**. What do you see?

```
10 PRINT "THEY PLAYED IN THE BAND."
15 PRINT "IT WAS A BEAUTIFUL HYMN."
20 PRINT "SHE WROTE MANY MELODIES."
25 PRINT "I LIKED CLASSICAL MUSIC."
30 PRINT "I PLAYED IN A ROCK BAND."
35 PRINT "THE BUGLE WOKE UP SALLY."
40 PRINT "SHE PLAYED THE BIG TUBA."
45 PRINT "THE DRUMS ARE VERY LOUD."
50 PRINT "SHE TAKES PIANO LESSONS."
55 PRINT "THE BAND HAD FIVE HORNS."
60 PRINT "THEY LIKE A JAZZY SOUND."
RUN
```

Computer Applications

INSTRUCTIONS

Enter each line twice.

Keep your eyes on the copy in the book.

EXERCISE 4

1Ø. 237 916 ØØ2 Ø26 235 92Ø 5Ø1 683
15. 344 241 9ØØ 765 628 672 745 38Ø
2Ø. 726 168 9Ø3 815 316 162 656 Ø51
25. 574 269 212 34Ø Ø51 25Ø 1Ø6 679
3Ø. 53Ø 578 754 795 928 214 992 587

EXERCISE 5

35. 6Ø2 562 684 546 Ø83 199 238 638
4Ø. 25Ø ØØ2 59Ø 513 97Ø Ø41 631 723
45. 958 257 258 283 181 239 959 4Ø8
5Ø. 72Ø Ø46 648 472 215 25Ø 782 216
55. Ø8Ø 43Ø 171 Ø59 634 789 672 5ØØ

EXERCISE 6

6Ø. 149 597 6Ø2 3Ø6 Ø33 582 7Ø3 297
65. 237 1ØØ 931 979 864 127 813 579
7Ø. 233 13Ø 493 729 936 166 653 852
75. 454 967 981 621 175 837 921 426
8Ø. 733 3ØØ 9Ø5 948 627 481 26Ø 788

INSTRUCTIONS

Enter the program on the right.

Correct any errors that you make when keyboarding this material.

To indent a paragraph 5 spaces, tap the **space bar** 5 times after you enter the first quotation mark.

USING THE PROGRAM

Now enter the word LIST. On separate lines, enter the numbers 50, 55, 60, 65, and 70. Do not put anything after each number, but press the **return key** after each number has been entered.

Enter the word LIST. What do you see?

Enter the word RUN. What do you see?

```
10 PRINT
15 PRINT
20 PRINT "     MARY AND MARIO WENT TO"
25 PRINT "THE ART SHOW LAST NIGHT.  I"
30 PRINT "TALKED TO MARY AT THE SHOW."
35 PRINT "SHE SAID THAT SHE LIKED THE"
40 PRINT "OIL PAINTINGS VERY MUCH."
45 PRINT
50 PRINT "     MARIO SPENT MANY HOURS"
55 PRINT "EXAMINING THE WATER COLORS"
60 PRINT "AT THE ART SHOW.  HE PAINTS"
65 PRINT "SOME WATER COLORS HIMSELF."
70 PRINT
75 PRINT "     WE ENJOYED THE POP ART"
80 PRINT "AT THE ART SHOW LAST NIGHT."
RUN
```

INSTRUCTIONS

Enter each line twice.

Keep your eyes on the copy in the book.

EXERCISE 7

1Ø. 627 493 579 438 457 646 942 471
15. 2Ø8 7Ø1 ØØ1 5Ø2 264 2Ø9 643 375
2Ø. Ø37 67Ø Ø97 Ø55 135 935 Ø29 237
25. 449 729 928 333 789 Ø45 Ø84 751
3Ø. 184 848 159 173 1Ø9 318 727 Ø72

EXCERCISE 8

35. 757 7Ø3 925 45Ø 297 697 874 489
4Ø. 931 795 718 3Ø3 794 785 31Ø Ø11
45. 299 Ø62 362 166 733 818 364 231
5Ø. Ø93 468 685 737 438 383 531 124
55. 581 153 55Ø 24Ø 695 883 824 761

EXERCISE 9

6Ø. 61Ø 5Ø9 911 211 177 974 492 771
65. 843 829 971 Ø15 641 984 932 64Ø
7Ø. 6Ø8 639 292 2Ø4 3Ø8 888 769 314
75. Ø27 496 835 663 784 129 923 696
8Ø. 851 3Ø9 Ø26 963 1Ø4 442 Ø12 6Ø7

INSTRUCTIONS

Enter the program on the right.

Correct any errors that you make when keyboarding this material.

USING THE PROGRAM

The first 2 commands to PRINT leave 2 blank lines before the first sentence is printed.

By inputting the command PRINT and nothing else on every second line, the sentences are double spaced on the screen.

Now enter the word LIST. On separate lines, enter the numbers 25, 35, 45, 55, 65, and 75. Press the **return key** after you enter each number.

Now enter the word LIST. What do you see on the screen?

Now enter the word RUN. What do you see on the screen?

```
10 PRINT
15 PRINT
20 PRINT "MARY WENT TO THE MOVIES."
25 PRINT
30 PRINT "THEIR PLAY WAS A COMEDY."
35 PRINT
40 PRINT "HE WROTE A MUSICAL PLAY."
45 PRINT
50 PRINT "THE TEACHER USED A FILM."
55 PRINT
60 PRINT "SHE BOUGHT A TELEVISION."
65 PRINT
70 PRINT "KIDS ENJOY PUPPET SHOWS."
75 PRINT
80 PRINT "THE BALLET IS BEAUTIFUL."
RUN
```

INSTRUCTIONS

Enter each line twice.

Keep your eyes on the copy in the book.

EXERCISE 10

```
1∅.  43.9  33.8  92.7  76.∅  8∅.7  7∅.9  83.8
15.  53.3  6∅.8  17.5  55.8  73.6  62.7  64.9
2∅.  16.6  29.2  28.9  67.2  81.∅  68.4  67.5
25.  43.∅  14.∅  12.9  7∅.∅  26.6  ∅9.6  53.5
3∅.  92.8  35.2  ∅7.∅  92.8  11.1  14.4  23.7
```

EXERCISE 11

```
35.  66.1  ∅9.1  ∅5.5  51.7  81.∅  27.5  2∅.2
4∅.  2∅.∅  22.7  ∅9.8  92.6  ∅7.8  55.4  24.4
45.  13.3  82.∅  58.7  63.9  4∅.3  12.6  28.4
5∅.  52.5  48.2  23.∅  37.4  87.4  43.7  97.7
55.  ∅6.1  98.4  64.9  89.7  59.1  25.3  ∅5.6
```

EXERCISE 12

```
6∅.  ∅∅.5  84.4  87.7  68.9  94.4  42.3  73.7
65.  65.6  84.8  74.2  94.3  58.4  95.2  57.3
7∅.  7∅.2  5∅.6  97.4  49.2  48.6  ∅9.6  54.3
75.  34.9  83.4  81.5  ∅7.1  99.7  64.3  6∅.∅
8∅.  62.9  53.5  23.2  ∅6.∅  92.∅  42.8  17.9
```

INSTRUCTIONS

Enter the program on the right.

Correct any errors that you make when keyboarding this material. A program will not work if it contains errors.

Do not put a line number in front of the word RUN.

Note: After you have entered and RUN the material, follow the instructions under *Using Your Program.*

USING THE PROGRAM

What do you see on the screen after you enter the word RUN?

How does this differ from the lines which you entered?

Now enter the word LIST. Do not put a number in front of the word LIST.

What do you see on the screen?

Now enter the word RUN again.

What do you see on the screen?

Press the **return key** after entering the word RUN or after entering the word LIST.

```
10 PRINT "GET A NEW BOOK FOR JOHN."
15 PRINT "THE TRAIN WAS VERY LATE."
20 PRINT "TAKE THE BUS TO TORONTO."
25 PRINT "I PAID TEN CENTS FOR IT."
30 PRINT "FATHER MADE A PEACH PIE."
35 PRINT "MAY DRINKS ORANGE JUICE."
40 PRINT "MARTY ENJOYS HAMBURGERS."
45 PRINT "I HAD JELLO FOR DESSERT."
50 PRINT "WASH YOUR DIRTY CLOTHES."
55 PRINT "GIVE ME YOUR NEW WALLET."
60 PRINT "SHE HAS A WARM RED VEST."
65 PRINT "SAM IS A GOOD POLICEMAN."
70 PRINT "HE HAS A PAIR OF GLOVES."
75 PRINT "JANET HAS A SORE THROAT."
80 PRINT "HE LIKES TO PLAY HOCKEY."
RUN
```

INSTRUCTIONS

Enter each line twice.

Keep your eyes on the copy in the book.

EXERCISE 13

```
1Ø.  72.71  63.71  33.65  38.44  13.65  23.26
15.  33.98  4Ø.42  49.2Ø  42.18  55.98  72.23
2Ø.  25.15  74.62  15.59  88.97  69.45  75.ØØ
25.  55.12  7Ø.83  79.87  82.89  76.16  96.23
3Ø.  47.41  98.39  87.72  34.6Ø  96.4Ø  53.54
```

EXERCISE 14

```
35.  1Ø.43  28.Ø4  21.49  99.21  2Ø.13  51.74
4Ø.  82.53  86.37  81.28  87.88  39.27  46.28
45.  36.23  13.76  16.86  45.86  85.25  52.Ø7
5Ø.  82.4Ø  65.Ø1  68.Ø7  61.Ø8  3Ø.44  93.26
55.  53.Ø7  82.51  12.56  25.65  57.5Ø  6Ø.59
```

EXERCISE 15

```
6Ø.  9Ø.77  66.98  25.Ø1  81.93  96.84  69.93
65.  96.35  71.13  1Ø.42  23.74  46.Ø9  77.48
7Ø.  32.97  7Ø.Ø4  65.66  41.12  34.79  37.11
75.  81.44  92.2Ø  96.98  68.96  4Ø.72  86.62
8Ø.  47.Ø8  32.32  74.93  73.Ø1  93.Ø6  86.43
```

Number Practice

INSTRUCTIONS

Enter each line twice.

Depress the **shift key** with the little finger of the hand not being used to enter the letter or character.

Hold down the **shift key**, enter the required letter or character, and then release the **shift key**.

Tap the **space bar** twice after a period at the end of a sentence.

```
1Ø Kate is ill.  Lead the lad fast.
15 Go home.  Go now.  Walk quickly.
2Ø Jess fed the fish.  Feed it now.
25 Use the rope.  I find it useful.
3Ø Fit the valve.  Jo needs it now.
35 Go to the gates.  Go there soon.
4Ø Go to the big department stores.
45 Dave likes pie.  Use the apples.
5Ø Visit Chan soon.  See Tang also.
55 Vivian and Alice went to Selma.
6Ø Glenda and Ken went skating too.
65 A bus went from Cypress to Ojai.
7Ø Fix the axle.  The car will run.
75 Help Tina repair her typewriter.
8Ø Vicksburg is a delightful place.
```

Upper and Lower Case Letters _____

WHEN USING A TYPEWRITER KEYBOARD, REMEMBER TO DE-PRESS THE **SHIFT LOCK** BEFORE ENTERING THE ALPHABETIC KEYS SINCE COMPUTERS USUALLY SHOW LETTERS IN UPPER CASE (CAPITAL LETTERS).

FINGER POSITION

- Place the left index finger on the F key and let the remaining fingers fall into place on the D, S, and A keys.
- Place the right index finger on the J key and let the remaining fingers fall into place on the K, L, and : keys.
- These keys are known as the *home row keys*.

INSTRUCTIONS

Enter each line twice.

Enter the line number at the beginning of each line. *Note:* A decimal is not needed after the line number when it is immediately followed by an alphabetic character.

Keep your eyes on the copy in the book.

Say each letter to yourself as you enter it.

Do not be concerned with errors at this time.

If time permits, practice exercises from the Number Practice section, pages 7-11.

```
1Ø  FFF  JJJ  FFF  JJJ  FFF  JJJ  FFF  JJJ
15  FFF  JJJ  FFF  JJJ  FJF  JFJ  FJF  JFJ
2Ø  DDD  KKK  DDD  KKK  DDD  KKK  DDD  KKK
25  DDD  KKK  DDD  KKK  DKD  KDK  DKD  KDK
3Ø  SSS  LLL  SSS  LLL  SSS  LLL  SSS  LLL
35  SSS  LLL  SSS  LLL  SLS  LSL  SLS  LSL
4Ø  AAA  :::  AAA  :::  AAA  :::  AAA  :::
45  AAA  :::  AAA  :::  A:A  :A:  A:A  :A:
5Ø  JA KA LA FA DA SA AJ AK ALL SAD
55  ALL SAD ADD ASK FALL DAD LAD AS
6Ø  FADS LASS FALL SALAD ASK AS SAD
65  SAD DADS: A SAD DAD: ASK A DAD:
```

Alphabetic Keys   A·S·D·F   J·K·L·:

KEYBOARDERS USING A TYPEWRITER KEYBOARD OR COM-
PUTER KEYBOARD THAT OUTPUTS IN BOTH UPPER AND
LOWER CASE LETTERS SHOULD DO PAGES 46 AND 47.

INSTRUCTIONS

Enter each line twice.

Depress the **shift key** with the little finger of the hand not being used to enter the letter or character.

Hold down the **shift key**, enter the required letter or character, and then release the **shift key**.

```
1Ø  Ron Sue Tom Wes Bob Ken Ike Jim
15  Harry Jackie Peter Mary Roberto
2Ø  Clifford Diane David Nancy Yuri
25  Allan Freda Nadina George Ernie
3Ø  Zeke Calvin Larry Orval Wes Mel
35  Austria Poland Norway Venezuela
4Ø  Germany Egypt Thailand Pakistan
45  Peru Korea Japan Italy Paraguay
5Ø  Hungary Morocco India Australia
55  Iran Bolivia China Spain Russia
6Ø  London Vienna Stockholm Hamburg
65  Newark Tempe Vancouver Valdosta
7Ø  Chicago Evanston Red Oaks Homer
75  Revere Yonkers Fairbanks Warren
8Ø  Westmont Elko Enid Bozeman Bend
85  Hampton Memphis Gallup Yorktown
```

Upper and Lower Case Letters

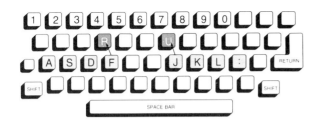

- Place the left index finger on the F key and let the remaining fingers fall into place on the D, S, and A keys.
- Place the right index finger on the J key and let the remaining fingers fall into place on the K, L, and : keys.
- Use the J finger to enter the U key.
- Use the F finger to enter the R key.

INSTRUCTIONS

Enter each line twice.

Keep your eyes on the copy in the book.

If time permits, practice exercises from the Number Practice section, pages 7-11.

```
1Ø  FFF JJJ DDD KKK SSS LLL AAA : : :
15  JUJ JUJ JUJ JUJ JUJ JUJ JUJ JUJ
2Ø  FU US DU JU UL SU FU US DU FULL
25  FULL DULL DUSK US USUAL AS FALL
3Ø  SKULL USUAL FULL DUSK DULL FULL
35  US FULL DULL SKULL USUAL SALADS
4Ø  FRF FRF FRF FRF FRF FRF FRF FRF
45  FRF JUJ FRF JUJ FRF JUJ FRF JUJ
5Ø  FAR JAR FAR JAR FAR JAR FAR JAR
55  DARK DUSK US ALL FAR SAD AS JAR
6Ø  ALL FAR SAD FALL FULL ADD SALAD
65  FAR JAR DAD SAD ASK ADD AS LASS
7Ø  FADS RADS JARS DARK DAD LAD ASK
75  A DARK JAR: A DULL SALAD: FULL:
```

Alphabetic Keys   R · U

TERMINOLOGY

> means is greater than

< means is less than

<> means not equal to

>= means greater than or equal to

<= means less than or equal to

↑ means exponentiation e.g., $4 \uparrow 3 = 4^3 = 4 \times 4 \times 4 = 64$, i.e., 4 times itself 3 times

$ declares variable name as a string

INSTRUCTIONS

Enter each line twice.

Correct any errors that you make when keyboarding this material.

Note: This is not a program and as such will not run.

```
10 READ X(1), X(2), X(3), X(4)
15 LET R = INT (1 + 6 * RND (0))
20 PRINT "NUMBER"; TAB(10); "TIMES APPEARING"
25 LET A(I) = A(I - 1)
30 LET A(I) = I * A(I -1)
35 PRINT X + (INT(1/2) + 1)
40 IF S(L)>S(I) THEN 120
45 IF X(15 * 15)<Y THEN 150
50 IF X<>200 THEN 80
55 IF Y>=125 THEN 120
60 IF Z<=150 THEN 230
65 LET X = 15↑2
70 LET W = (4 + 9/3)↑2
75 READ A$
80 IF A$ = "END" THEN 140
```

Special Characters in BASIC ⎯⎯⎯⎯⎯⎯⎯⎯⎯⎯⎯⎯⎯⎯⎯⎯⎯ 45

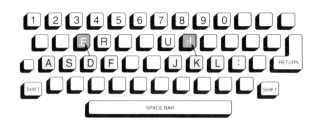

FINGER POSITION

- Place the left hand fingers on the F, D, S, and A keys and the right hand fingers on the J, K, L, and : keys.
- Use the K finger to enter the I key.
- Use the D finger to enter the E key.

INSTRUCTIONS

Enter each line twice.

Do not be concerned with errors at this time.

If time permits, practice exercises from the Number Practice section, pages 7-11.

```
1Ø FFF JJJ DDD KKK SSS LLL AAA : : :
15 JUJ FRF JUJ FRF UJU RFR UJU RFR
2Ø KIK KIK KIK KIK KIK KIK KIK KIK
25 ID IL IR IS IK IF DI FI KI FILL
3Ø IS DID ILL FILL KILL KISS SAILS
35 AIR LID KID SKIS LAID DID FAILS
4Ø DED DED DED DED DED DED DED DED
45 EA ED ER ES EL RE SE KE DE DEER
5Ø ARE EAR RED SEE USE DESK SLIDES
55 RIDE DRESS FEEL LAKES DEER FREE
6Ø DIE DIES DIED USE SLIDE SEE ARE
65 FELL RAKE RUDE RULER SEEDS LEAF
7Ø SEE FREE FEEL DEAL FIRES IS EAR
75 LAKE RAKES LIFE DEER FELL FIRES
```

FINGER POSITION

When entering special characters, keep your fingers on the F, D, S, A and J, K, L, : keys or on the numeric home row keys and enter the special character with the closest finger.

TERMINOLOGY

= means equal or replace with

+ means add

− means subtract

* means multiply

/ means divide

( ) Brackets have the same meaning as they do in arithmetic; i.e., the computer will do the operation inside the brackets first.

, Instructs the computer to read each number separately.

INSTRUCTIONS

Enter each line twice.

Correct any errors that you make when keyboarding this material.

Note: This is not a program and as such will not run.

```
10 LET S = 14.7 + 15.2
15 LET M = 250 - 125
20 LET X = 15 * 15
25 LET Y = 225/15
30 LET P = 50 * 7.50
35 LET A = P - 60.67
40 LET C = S/4
45 LET D = .10 * P + .058 * P
50 LET X = (A + B)/2
55 INPUT P, R, T
60 LET I = P * R * T
65 DATA 32, 45, 56, 67
70 PRINT "COST = $"; C
75 PRINT "PROFIT = $"; P
80 PRINT "BID = $"; B
```

Special Characters in BASIC _____ 44

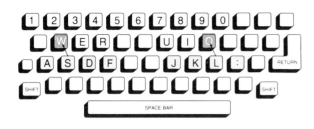

- Place your fingers on the home row keys.
- Use the L finger to enter the O key.
- Use the S finger to enter the W key.

INSTRUCTIONS

Enter each line twice.

Keep your eyes on the copy in the book.

Say each letter to yourself as you enter it.

If time permits, practice exercises from the Number Practice section, pages 7-11.

```
1Ø  FFF JJJ DDD KKK SSS LLL AAA ::: 
15  FRF JUJ DED KIK RFR UJU EDE IKI
2Ø  LOL LOL LOL LOL LOL LOL LOL LOL
25  OL OR OK OU OF OD OS OA DO DOOR
3Ø  DOOR LOOK FOOD OLD DOLL SOLDIER
35  FOUR ROAD ROLL ROSE SOFA FLOORS
4Ø  DOLLAR LOOSE FORK FOLD DO OLDER
45  SWS SWS SWS SWS SWS SWS SWS SWS
5Ø  WA WI WO WE WL AW OW EW SW OWLS
55  SAW DRAW WALK WILL WOLF WOOD WE
6Ø  WORK FEW WAS WAKE WALL WEEK WAS
65  WEEDS WIFE FLOWER WALRUS WE SAW
7Ø  WEAK WEAR WIRE WIDE WOOL FLOWER
75  WOKE WORDS AWAKE WELL WERE FOWL
```

FINGER POSITION

When entering special characters, keep your fingers on the F, D, S, A and J, K, L, : keys *or* on the numeric home row keys and enter the special character with the closest finger.

TERMINOLOGY

THEN means that if the condition in the preceding IF statement is met, then the computer jumps to a specified line number e.g. line 15. In the two DATA statements, lines 35 and 40, the numbers are read alternately into R and H, (line 30), i.e., 4.65 into R, 32 into H, 3.75 into R, 40 into H, 4.25 into R etc.

INSTRUCTIONS

Enter each line twice.

Correct any errors that you make when keyboarding this material.

Note: This is not a program and as such will not run.

```
5  LET A = 2.
10 LET X = (A + B)/(A - B)
15 IF A = B THEN 80
20 PRINT X; " IS A NEGATIVE NUMBER"
25 IF P * Q = R * S THEN 150
30 READ R, H
35 DATA 4.65, 32, 3.75, 40
40 DATA 4.25, 36, 4.50, 34
45 PRINT "GROSS PAY IS $"; P
50 FOR M = 1 TO 6
55 INPUT A, B, C
60 READ I, N, J
65 PRINT "THE ANSWER IS "; A
70 PRINT TAB(15); "NO. SOLD"
75 PRINT TAB(30); "UNIT PRICE"
80 PRINT TAB(45); "$ SALES"
```

Special Characters in BASIC _____

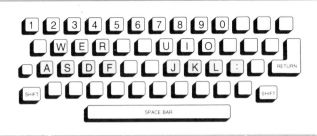

INSTRUCTIONS

Enter each line twice.

Keep your eyes on the copy at all times.

Say each letter to yourself as you enter it.

Do not be concerned with errors at this time.

If time permits, practice exercises from the Number Practice section, pages 7-11.

```
10 FFF JJJ DDD KKK SSS LLL AAA :::
15 FRF JUJ DED KIK SWS LOL SWS LOL
20 ALL ARE DID EAR FAR OLD RED SAD
25 DOE USE SAW SEE ASK WAS AIR RED
30 ILL LOW OWL ARE DIE ADD DAD FAD
35 FALL FEED FIRE FORK WOODS RIDES
40 FULL LIKE LOOK DEER ROADS READS
45 DARK DESK FOUR WORD WALKS SORES
50 LOUD READ RIDE SLOW FLOWS WORKS
55 DIES OWLS JOKE DUSK FEWER WEEKS
60 FEAR DEAR WEAK LEAK WALLS FOULS
65 WE SEE SALADS: OLD FLOWERS DIE:
70 RED DESK: FOUR WORDS: OLD OWLS:
75 WE LOOK SAD: WE READ OLD WORDS:
```

Alphabetic Keys – Review

INSTRUCTIONS

Enter each line twice.

Correct any errors that you make when keyboarding these words.

Keep your eyes on the copy in your book.

Practice these words until you can keyboard them at a rate of 4 to 5 lines in 1 minute.

```
10 FOR FOR FOR FOR FOR FOR FOR FOR
15 DIM DIM DIM DIM DIM DIM DIM DIM
20 RND RND RND RND RND RND RND RND
25 INT INT INT INT INT INT INT INT
30 NEXT NEXT NEXT NEXT NEXT NEXT
35 STOP STOP STOP STOP STOP STOP
40 SAVE SAVE SAVE SAVE SAVE SAVE
45 LOAD LOAD LOAD LOAD LOAD LOAD
50 GOTO GOTO GOTO GOTO GOTO GOTO
55 GOSUB GOSUB GOSUB GOSUB GOSUB
60 RETURN RETURN RETURN RETURN
65 IF THEN IF THEN IF THEN IF THEN
70 MAT READ MAT READ MAT READ
75 MAT PRINT MAT PRINT MAT PRINT
```

FINGER POSITION

- Place your fingers on the home row keys.
- Use the J finger to enter the H key.
- Use the F finger to enter the G key.

INSTRUCTIONS

Enter each line twice.

Keep your eyes on the copy in the book.

Do not be concerned with errors at this time.

If time permits, practice exercises from the Number Practice section, pages 7-11.

```
1Ø  JJJ JUJ JJJ JUJ JJJ JUJ JJJ JUJ
15  JHJ JHJ JHJ JHJ JHJ JHJ JHJ JHJ
2Ø  JUJ JHJ JUJ JHJ JUJ JHJ JUJ JHJ
25  HE HI HO HA HR SH WH HE HI HILL
3Ø  HAS HARD HEAR HOW WASH HIS HALF
35  RUSH HOOK HEEL HIDE WISH WHALES
4Ø  FFF FRF FFF FRF FFF FRF FFF FRF
45  FGF FGF FRF FGF FRF FGF FRF FGF
5Ø  FRF FGF FRF FGF FRF FGF FRF FGF
55  GO GU GA GL GI GR GS GH OG DOGS
6Ø  DIG FOG EGG RUG WAG LEG DOG LOG
65  GROW FLAG FROG GIRL GOLD GARAGE
7Ø  OUR OLD HOUSE: SLOW OLD HORSES:
75  ROUGH WEEDS GROW: SEE OUR EGGS:
```

Alphabetic Keys   G · H

These are some of the **command words** in the computer language called BASIC. It is important that you are able to input these words quickly and accurately.

INSTRUCTIONS

Enter each line twice.

Keep your eyes on the copy in the book.

Correct any errors that you make when keyboarding these words.

Practice these words until you can keyboard them at a rate of 4 to 5 lines in 1 minute.

```
10 REM REM REM REM REM REM REM REM
15 NEW NEW NEW NEW NEW NEW NEW NEW
20 END END END END END END END END
25 RUN RUN RUN RUN RUN RUN RUN RUN
30 LET LET LET LET LET LET LET LET
35 LIST LIST LIST LIST LIST LIST
40 READ READ READ READ READ READ
45 PEEK PEEK PEEK PEEK PEEK PEEK
50 POKE POKE POKE POKE POKE POKE
55 DATA DATA DATA DATA DATA DATA
60 INPUT INPUT INPUT INPUT INPUT
65 PRINT PRINT PRINT PRINT PRINT
70 CLOSE CLOSE CLOSE CLOSE CLOSE
75 SCRATCH SCRATCH SCRATCH SCRATCH
```

BASIC Computer Language Words _____

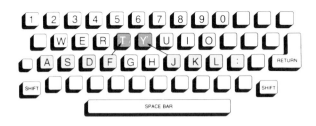

FINGER POSITION

- Place your fingers on the home row keys.
- Use the J finger to enter the Y key.
- Use the F finger to enter the T key.

INSTRUCTIONS

Enter each line twice.

Keep your eyes on the copy in your book.

If time permits, practice exercises from the Number Practice section, pages 7-11.

```
1Ø  JUJ  JHJ  JUJ  JHJ  JUJ  JHJ  JUJ  JHJ
15  JYJ  JYJ  JYJ  JYJ  JYJ  JYJ  JYJ  JYJ
2Ø  JHJ  JYJ  JHJ  JYJ  JHJ  JYJ  JHJ  JYJ
25  YE  YO  AY  EY  LY  KY  DY  RY  SY  EYES
3Ø  FLY  SKY  YES  DRY  WAY  LAY  HAY  SAY
35  UGLY  SORRY  YELLOW  HURRY  HIGHWAY
4Ø  FOGGY  YARD  KEYS  DAISY  SILLY  YES
45  FRF  FGF  FRF  FGF  FRF  FGF  FRF  FGF
5Ø  FTF  FTF  FTF  FTF  FTF  FTF  FTF  FTF
55  FGF  FTF  FGF  FTF  FGF  FTF  FGF  FTF
6Ø  TI  TA  TO  TR  TE  TU  TH  OT  AT  HATS
65  ATE  EAT  FAT  GET  HOT  SIT  TIE  WET
7Ø  SALT  SHUT  TEETH  DIRTY  FRUIT  HIS
75  LETTER  LITTER  TART  START  STORKS
```

Alphabetic Keys   T · Y

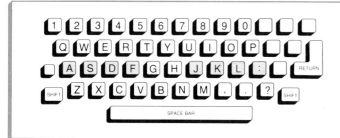

INSTRUCTIONS

Enter each line twice.

Keep your eyes on the copy in the book.

Correct any errors that you make when keyboarding these sentences.

Try to keyboard 3 to 4 lines correctly in 1 minute.

```
1Ø THE CONVEYOR IN THE PLANT BROKE.
15 THEY WATCHED TELEVISION ALL DAY.
2Ø MOM READ THE KIDS A SHORT STORY.
25 THE STOWAWAYS HID NEAR THE DOOR.
3Ø SUE PUT HER BOOKS IN HER LOCKER.
35 THE FULLBACK SCORED A TOUCHDOWN.
4Ø CATS AND RABBITS MAKE NICE PETS.
45 TREES ARE PLANTED TO GIVE SHADE.
5Ø THE THIRD OF JULY WAS A HOT DAY.
55 I DISCOVERED A LEAK IN THE PIPE.
6Ø THEY GET LIGHT FROM THE LANTERN.
65 WE LIVE ALL ALONE ON THE ISLAND.
7Ø OLD GRIZZLY BEARS ARE DANGEROUS.
75 A NEW COAT OF PAINT WAS APPLIED.
8Ø I HAD TO FIND TWO SIMILAR SOCKS.
```

Alphabetic Practice

INSTRUCTIONS

Enter each line twice.

Say each letter to yourself as you enter it.

Keep your eyes on the copy at all times.

If time permits, practice exercises from the Number Practice section, pages 7-11.

```
10 JUJ FRF KIK DED LOL SWS LOL SWS
15 JUJ JHJ JYJ FRF FGF FTF JYJ FTF
20 JYJ FTF JYJ FTF JYJ FTF JYJ FTF
25 ALL ARE ATE DID DOG DRY EAR FAR
30 WAS HAS LAD FOG LOG JOG TAG DAY
35 THE HOT SAD HAD JUG DIG YES SAW
40 DEER DESK DOOR DRAW DIRTY TIGER
45 EYES FALL TOYS WASH DRESS TREES
50 DESK WORK FEED GIRL WATER WHITE
55 FEED LAKE FOUR DEAR TODAY HEART
60 GREW GROW FLOW JUTE EIGHT TOAST
65 FAKE FEAR YEAR FULL HORSE KITES
70 WE FLY KITES AT THE LAKE TODAY:
75 A SAD DAY: EAT TOAST: TEST HER:
```

Alphabetic Keys – Review

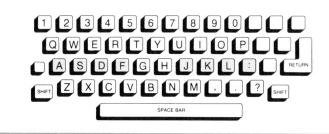

INSTRUCTIONS

Enter each line twice.

Keep your eyes on the copy in the book.

Correct any errors that you make when keyboarding these sentences.

How many lines can you keyboard in 1 minute? In 2 minutes?

```
10  DID UNICORNS EVER LIVE ON EARTH?
15  THE POULTRY FARMER RAISED DUCKS.
20  I HEARD SOMEONE CRYING FOR HELP.
25  THE FOOTBALL FELT SOMEWHAT FLAT.
30  THE RIVER WAS NOT VERY STRAIGHT.
35  PAUL DID THE DISHES FOR HIS MOM.
40  THEY WISHED TO VACATION IN PERU.
45  NUCLEAR ENERGY IS CONTROVERSIAL.
50  JO WENT TO THE ZOO TO SEE A GNU.
55  RAIN FELL GENTLY ON THE PLATEAU.
60  WHERE CAN I GO TO GET SOME FOOD?
65  RAOUL HAD HAMBURGERS FOR SUPPER.
70  ELLA CLOSED THE DOOR BEHIND HER.
75  ON THURSDAY I GO TO THE LIBRARY.
80  I LISTENED TO THE RECITAL ALONE.
```

Alphabetic Practice

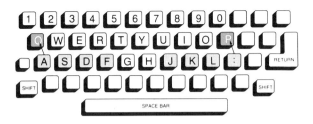

FINGER POSITION

- Place your fingers on the home row keys.
- Use the : finger to enter the P key.
- Use the A finger to enter the Q key.

INSTRUCTIONS

Enter each line twice.

Keep your elbows by your side when entering the P and Q.

Keep your eyes on the copy in the book.

If time permits, practice exercises from the Number Practice section, pages 7-11.

```
1Ø  FFF JJJ DDD KKK SSS LLL AAA : :
15  :P: :P: :P: :P: :P: :P: :P: :P:
2Ø  PL PO PU PE PL PA IP AP LP PEAR
25  PIE PIG POP PUT RIP TAP TIP PET
3Ø  PAY PAD LIP SIP TIP POT TOP HOP
35  HELP SKIP SOAP PUSH APPLE PAPER
4Ø  PEPPER SLIPPERS HAPPY TAP PUPPY
45  FFF JJJ DDD KKK SSS LLL AAA : :
5Ø  AQA AQA AQA AQA AQA AQA AQA AQA
55  QU SQ QU SQ QU SQ QU SQ QU AQUA
6Ø  QUAD QUAY QUID QUIP QUAIL QUAKE
65  QUIT QUOTE EQUAL QUAINT REQUIRE
7Ø  QUARREL SQUARES QUARTER SQUALID
75  QUARTET LIQUIDS QUIETLY EQUATOR
```

Alphabetic Keys Q · P

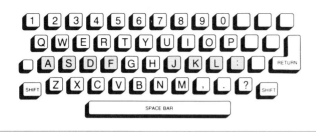

INSTRUCTIONS

Enter each line twice.

Keep your eyes on the copy in the book.

Correct any errors that you make when keyboarding these sentences.

How many lines can you keyboard correctly in 1 minute? Each line contains the equivalent of 7 words. Consequently, 1 line equals 7 words; 2 lines equal 14 words; 3 lines equal 21 words; 4 lines equal 28 words, etc.

10 HE GOT A NEW RUG IN HIS BEDROOM.

15 JIM HAS TO WASH AND WAX THE CAR.

20 HE KEPT HIS GLASSES IN A DRAWER.

25 HER MOTHER NEEDED A HEARING AID.

30 SHE WORE A BRIGHT ORANGE BLOUSE.

35 GINGER WANTED TO BE A PUPPETEER.

40 WHY DID WE HAVE TO GO WITH THEM?

45 THE LITTLE BOY DETESTED SPINACH.

50 THE PAN WAS LOST IN THE KITCHEN.

55 I ENJOYED LISTENING TO THE OBOE.

60 THE ILLUSTRATOR HAD MUCH TALENT.

65 THAT ANGLER CAUGHT SEVERAL FISH.

70 JANET LIVED NEAR HER CLASSMATES.

75 THE HATCHERY WAS NEAR THE RIVER.

80 MY BASEMENT IS CHILLY IN WINTER.

Alphabetic Practice

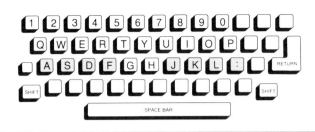

INSTRUCTIONS

Enter each line twice.

Keep your eyes on the copy in your book.

After you have practiced the lines, try to enter the last 3 lines in this exercise in 1 minute. If you can do this, you are keyboarding at a rate of 21 gross words per minute (GWPM). *Note:* Each line contains keystrokes that equal 7 words.

```
1Ø FRF JUJ DED KIK SWS LOL AQA :P:
15 RFR UJU EDE IKI WSW OLO QAQ P:P
2Ø FRF JUJ FGF JHJ FTF JYJ FTF JYJ
25 AQA :P: AQA :P: QAQ P:P QAQ P:P
3Ø ALL ASH DAD FAD GAG GAS JOG LAD
35 ADD ASK SAG EWE EYE TIE IRE TIP
4Ø ORE TOE TOP PET TOW PIE TOY WET
45 DASH FALL FLAG GALL GLASS SLASH
5Ø PIER TIRE PIPE TOUR PUPPY POWER
55 TYPE PUTT QUIP ROPE POPPY QUOTE
6Ø HOPE LEFT PUSH QUIT SHIPS QUIET
65 HE ATE THE PEAR: FLY THE KITES:
7Ø WASH THE DIRTY DISH: GO TO HER:
75 RAKE THE GRASS: EAT THE FRUITS:
```

Alphabetic Keys – Review

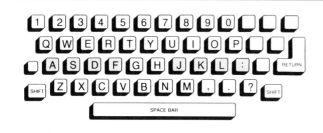

INSTRUCTIONS

Enter each line twice.

Keep your eyes on the copy in the book.

Correct any errors that you make when keyboarding these sentences.

10 THE MEASLES MADE ME STAY IN BED.

15 THERE WAS CONFUSION IN THE ROOM.

20 THE STRANGER HAD A SLENDER BODY.

25 HE DID THE DIFFICULT JOB SLOWLY.

30 WHY DID THEY WANT TO GO SO LATE?

35 WITH A LITTLE AID YOU CAN DO IT.

40 UNDERSTAND WHAT WAS SAID TO HER.

45 CHILDREN HATE SOUR TASTING FOOD.

50 SUE SOLD CANDIES FOR THE SCHOOL.

55 WE HAD COD FOR OUR SEAFOOD MEAL.

60 THEY WENT TO EAT IN THE KITCHEN.

65 THE OLD COUPLE LIVED IN A HOUSE.

70 MOTHER HAD TO REPAIR THE AWNING.

75 ED FOUND THE SPEECH VERY BORING.

80 THE LEPRECHAUN SAVED THE CASTLE.

Alphabetic Practice _____ 37

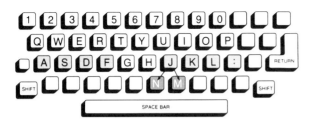

FINGER POSITION

- Place your fingers on the home row keys.
- Use the J finger to enter the M key.
- Use the J finger to enter the N key.

INSTRUCTIONS

Enter each line twice.

Do not be concerned with errors at this time.

If time permits, practice exercises from the Number Practice section, pages 7-11.

```
1Ø  JJJ  JUJ  JHJ  JYJ  JJJ  JUJ  JHJ  JYJ
15  JMJ  JMJ  JMJ  JMJ  JMJ  JMJ  JMJ  JMJ
2Ø  MA  ME  MI  MO  OM  IM  UM  RM  SM  MILK
25  ARM  JAM  MAP  MAT  MOP  MET  SUM  MUG
3Ø  MAKE  MORE  SOME  SWIM  MOUTH  MOUSE
35  FARM  GAME  LAMP  DAMP  MITTS  MAKES
4Ø  JNJ  JNJ  JNJ  JNJ  JNJ  JNJ  JNJ  JNJ
45  JMJ  JNJ  JMJ  JNJ  JMJ  JNJ  JMJ  JNJ
5Ø  JUJ  JHJ  JYJ  JMJ  JNJ  JMJ  JNJ  JMJ
55  NO  NE  NA  NY  NK  NK  NT  AN  EN  MANE
6Ø  HEN  NEW  RUN  SON  AND  GUN  MAN  RAN
65  NAIL  NAME  RAIN  SNOW  PANTS  NURSE
7Ø  MIND  MINE  MOAN  MANY  HUMAN  MANLY
75  MENU  HYMN  NORM  MEAN  LINEN  ONION
```

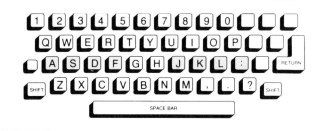

INSTRUCTIONS

Enter each line twice.

Keep your eyes on the copy in the book.

Correct any errors that you make when keyboarding these sentences.

```
1Ø I SAW THE STAR WITH A TELESCOPE.
15 DAD PREPARED A DELICIOUS DINNER.
2Ø THE LARGE BLACK HORSE RAN ALONE.
25 THE GAUGE WAS NOT VERY ACCURATE.
3Ø ED WAS JUST BEGINNING HIS ESSAY.
35 PIA DOUBTED THE NEWSPAPER STORY.
4Ø THE AUTHOR WAS SIGNING HER BOOK.
45 JOY WAS LEARNING TO FLY A BLIMP.
5Ø I VOTED IN THE NATIONAL ELECTION.
55 FATHER DID THE JOB WITH A DRILL.
6Ø A CYLINDER IS A GEOMETRIC SHAPE.
65 SID WORSHIPPED AT THE CATHEDRAL.
7Ø THE ROBBER WAS BROUGHT TO TRIAL.
75 THE CHILD PLAYED WITH HIS JACKS.
8Ø THE CASHIER LOST TWENTY DOLLARS.
```

Alphabetic Practice

FINGER POSITION

- Place your fingers on the home row keys.
- Use the F finger to enter the V key.
- Use the F finger to enter the B key.

INSTRUCTIONS

Enter each line twice.

Say each letter to yourself as you enter it.

Keep your eyes on the copy in the book.

If time permits, practice exercises from the Number Practice section, pages 7-11.

```
1Ø  FFF FRF FGF FTF FFF FRF FGF FTF
15  FVF FVF FVF FVF FVF FVF FVF FVF
2Ø  VE VI VY AV IV EV VE VI VY FIVE
25  EVE VAN VAT VET VOW IVY VIE EVE
3Ø  HAVE GIVE DIVE GAVE RIVER VISIT
35  VASE SAVE HIVE FIVE HEAVY EVERY
4Ø  FBF FBF FBF FBF FBF FBF FBF FBF
45  FVF FBF FVF FBF FVF FBF FVF FBF
5Ø  FRF FGF FTF FVF FBF FVF FBF FVF
55  BA BE BI BY BR BU BO AB OB BIRD
6Ø  BAD BED BEE BAR ROB SOB BUS BIG
65  BEAR BIKE BIRD BLOW BIBLE BROWN
7Ø  BLUE BOOK BOAT BEEN RABBITS BAT
75  BEAVER BUBBLE PEBBLE BEAR BLOOD
```

Alphabetic Keys   V · B

INSTRUCTIONS

Enter each line twice.

Keep your eyes on the copy in the book.

Correct any errors that you make when keyboarding these sentences.

10 THE KING LIVES IN AN OLD CASTLE.

15 THE SALMON TOOK THE MINNOW BAIT.

20 I ENJOY WATCHING MY PET TURTLES.

25 PAULA KEPT AN ANT FARM IN A JAR.

30 MIKE BROKE HIS LEG WHILE SKIING.

35 SIXTEEN PLUS FOURTEEN IS THIRTY.

40 ANNE GOES TO THE LAUNDRY WEEKLY.

45 THAT PHYSICIAN HELPS ALL PEOPLE.

50 THE FARMER WAS USING HIS HARROW.

55 JOE SAID HE HAD A SORE SHOULDER.

60 FIREFIGHTERS USE FOAM ON A FIRE.

65 MARY WAS A GOOD MEDICAL STUDENT.

70 THE PRAIRIE HAS FLAT, ARID LAND.

75 A LIGHTHOUSE OVERLOOKED THE SEA.

80 FROM THE QUIET CROWD CAME A CRY.

Alphabetic Practice

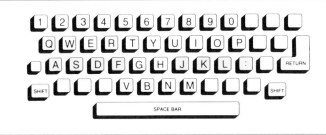

INSTRUCTIONS

Enter each line twice.

After you have practiced the lines, try to enter the last 4 lines in this exercise in 1 minute. If you can do this, you are keyboarding at a rate of 28 gross words per minute (GWPM).

```
10 FRF JUJ DED KIK SWS LOL AQA :P:
15 JUJ JHJ JYJ JMJ JNJ JMJ JNJ JMJ
20 FRF FGF FTF FVF FBF FVF FBF FVF
25 ALL ASH BAG BAN DAB DAM FAN GAG
30 BAND BANE KNOB NIBS BEVEL VALVE
35 BONE BOON BRAN BUNK MASON MOUND
40 BURN BINS BONG SNOB MINER MINOR
45 BABE DOVE DIVE BLOB MELON MONEY
50 VETO OVEN VIEW VINE MAUVE WEAVE
55 QUOTA QUEER QUEEN QUAKE QUARREL
60 WAVE GLOVE GRAVY STONE VAN VOLE
65 PUT THE BOOK THERE: EAT APPLES:
70 WASH THE BIG DOG: WASH THE POT:
75 THE SHEEP ATE OATS: RUN TO HER:
```

INSTRUCTIONS

Enter each line twice.

Correct any errors that you make when keyboarding these sentences.

Keep your eyes on the copy in the book.

```
1Ø JOSE PLANTED A SEED BY THE LANE.
15 THE STORM BROUGHT WIND AND RAIN.
2Ø BONN IS BEAUTIFUL IN THE SPRING.
25 THE CUBS WENT WITH THEIR MOTHER.
3Ø GARY IS BEAUTIFUL IN THE SPRING.
35 I DECIDED NOT TO RIDE THE HORSE
4Ø THE PRETTIEST MARBLE WAS YELLOW.
45 NICOLE USED A NET TO CATCH FISH.
5Ø WE WATCHED THE BIRD GLIDE ALONG.
55 ERIK SAW CHIMPANZEES AT THE ZOO.
6Ø THE WORMS WERE EATEN BY THE OWL.
65 THEY SKIPPED STONES ON THE LAKE.
7Ø MAY I DRIVE TO CULLMAN, ALABAMA?
75 CAROLYN WAS JUMPING UP AND DOWN.
8Ø IT IS NICE ON A FAIR DAY AT SEA.
```

Alphabetic Practice

- Place your fingers on the home row keys.
- Use the D finger to enter the C key.
- Use the S finger to enter the X key.

INSTRUCTIONS

Enter each line twice.

Do not be concerned with errors at this time.

Keep your eyes on the copy in the book.

If time permits, practice exercises from the Number Practice section, pages 7-11.

```
1Ø  DCD DCD DCD DCD DCD DCD DCD DCD
15  DED DCD DED DCD DED DCD DED DCD
2Ø  CA CR CU CO CH CE CK CL AC DUCK
25  CAR COW CUT CAT CAP COT ACE CUE
3Ø  CAKE COLD COME CORN JUICE CHALK
35  FACE SICK ROCK RACE CLIMB CAMEL
4Ø  CITY LACE DUCK COST CANDY CLOCK
45  SXS SXS SXS SXS SXS SXS SXS SXS
5Ø  SWS SXS SWS SXS SWS SXS SWS SXS
55  IX OX EX AX XI XT IX OX EX TAXI
6Ø  BOX FOX MIX SIX FIX AXE HEX WAX
65  EXIT TEXT FLUX LYNX EXILE EXTRA
7Ø  JINX MINX AXLE NEXT INDEX SIXTY
75  MAXIM LATEX OXBOW CRUX OXEN FIX
```

INSTRUCTIONS

Enter each line twice.

Keep your eyes on the copy in the book.

Correct any errors that you make when keyboarding these sentences.

Try to keyboard the last 3 lines in 1 minute. Correct all errors. If you can do this, you are keyboarding at a rate of 21 net words per minute (wpm).

```
1Ø WE GET TUNGSTEN FROM THE GROUND.
15 CLEAR THE SNOW FROM THE WALKWAY.
2Ø SHE PLANNED TO SAIL ON THE LAKE.
25 WHY DOES THE WATER APPEAR BROWN?
3Ø WE WERE FASCINATED BY THE STARS.
35 THE SWAMP WAS FULL OF MOSQUITOS.
4Ø THE TEXT WAS STUDIED BY WILLIAM.
45 THE MAN AND WOMAN WERE VERY ILL.
5Ø THE ASH IN THE FIRE WAS GLOWING.
55 SNOW FELL SOFTLY IN THE MORNING.
6Ø DECEMBER WAS MY FAVORITE MONTH.
65 THAT STAR GLOWS ONLY VERY DIMLY.
7Ø THE SINGER HAD A POWERFUL VOICE.
75 THIS FOOD SHOULD LAST FIVE DAYS.
8Ø THE LAKE IS WARMER THAN THE SEA.
```

Alphabetic Practice

WHEN THIS LESSON IS COMPLETED, THE USER SHOULD BE ABLE TO ENTER ANY ALPHABETIC KEY ON A TYPEWRITER OR COMPUTER KEYBOARD WHILE KEEPING HIS/HER EYES ON THE COPY IN THE BOOK.

FINGER POSITION

- Place your fingers on the home row keys.
- Use the A finger to enter the Z key.

INSTRUCTIONS

Enter each line twice.

Practice the last 4 lines in this exercise until you can input them in 1 minute with no more than 2 errors. If you can do this, you are keyboarding at 28 gross words per minute (GWPM).

```
1Ø  AZA AZA AZA AZA AZA AZA AZA AZA
15  AQA AZA AQA AZA AQA AZA AQA AZA
2Ø  ZOO FEZ CZAR DAZE HAZE MAZE ZOO
25  ZINC ZONE ZERO COZY LAZY PUZZLE
3Ø  DOZEN PRIZE BUZZ JAZZ ZOOM OOZE
35  BLIZZARD PIZZA BAZAAR SIZE ZANY
4Ø  CRUX QUAD JACK CZAR FUNDS WANDS
45  STAR FLAX QUAY JUMP DAZED CAVES
5Ø  HOLY WIGS BONE HAWK PLOTS HOPES
55  MEAN PAWN AXIS QUID JADES VESTS
6Ø  OILY RAKE GIFT BARN CLUBS COMBS
65  MEAT GOWN FLUX QUIP VIEWS HIKES
7Ø  JUNK MAZE CAKE FINE AXLES JAILS
75  LOVE UGLY BEST HARD CONES QUITS
```

Alphabetic Keys   Z

INSTRUCTIONS

Enter each line twice.

Correct any errors that you make when keyboarding these sentences.

Keep your eyes on the copy in your book.

10 JOAN PLAYS THIRD BASE VERY WELL.

15 I SAW THE GHOST IN THE OLD HOME.

20 THE OLD FARMER STILL GREW GRAIN.

25 THE COIN WAS FOUND BY THAT TREE.

30 DID THE DUKE GET HIS STRONG TEA?

35 THE STRANGER HAD TWO GOLD TEETH.

40 WHEN CAN WE GO FOR A QUICK SWIM?

45 REPLAY THE SONG A LITTLE LOUDER.

50 WE GO TO A SCHOOL FOR BOYS ONLY.

55 GUM COST TEN CENTS AT THE STORE.

60 THEY DRIVE TO THAT LAKE TO FISH.

65 HOW OLD MUST YOU NOW BE TO VOTE?

70 THE TRAIN FARE IS EIGHT DOLLARS.

75 THE GUESTS WERE TO EAT AT SEVEN.

80 HE GAVE THE GIRL A NICE PRESENT.

Alphabetic Practice

WHEN USING A TYPEWRITER KEYBOARD TO SIMULATE A COM-PUTER KEYBOARD, GO TO PAGE 28.

This exercise shows you how to correct some simple errors that might be made when entering information on a computer keyboard. (Numeric errors are corrected in the same way.) *Note:* If the computer does not have **insert** and **delete keys,** check the User's Manual to see how to make corrections.

The key statement is:

10 MARY WENT TO VISIT FRIENDS.

Enter the following:

10 MARY WENT TO VISIT FRE

You notice immediately that you entered the E and not the I. Press the **delete key** once and enter the I and finish entering the line.

10 MARY WENT TO VISIT FREINDS.

The I and E in FRIENDS have been interchanged. Move the **cursor** (point of printing on the screen usually shown by a flashing indicator) to the E in FREINDS and enter the keys I and E. Press the **return key.**

10 MARY WENT VISIT FRIENDS.

You have omitted the word TO. Move the **cursor** to the V in VISIT and tap the **insert key** three times (once for the T, O, and the space that follows the word). Enter the word TO and press the **return key.**

10 MARY WENT TO VISSIT FRIENDS.

Move the **cursor** to the second S in VISSIT and press the **delete key** once. Now press the **return key.**

10 MSTY ERNY YO BIDIY GTIRNFD.

Move the **cursor** to the M at the beginning of the line. Enter the correct line in its entirety. Press the **return key.**

Correcting Errors on a Computer Keyboard ⎯⎯⎯⎯⎯⎯⎯⎯⎯⎯⎯⎯⎯⎯⎯

INSTRUCTIONS

Enter each line twice.

Keep your eyes on the copy in your book.

Correct any errors that you make when keyboarding these sentences.

```
1Ø MARY IS A GOOD FRIEND TO MY DAD.
15 SNOW AND RAIN FELL ON THE BARNS.
2Ø HE PAID TEN DOLLARS FOR THE JAR.
25 WE WENT TO SCHOOL WITH HIS DOGS.
3Ø JOHN PAID OUR BILLS AT THE BANK.
35 PLAY THE TAPES ONCE MORE FOR ME.
4Ø AN OLD MAN LIVED NEAR THE GROVE.
45 JOE THREW THE FOOTBALL VERY FAR.
5Ø I HAVE AN INTEREST IN CHEMISTRY.
55 THE BIG BEAVERS ARE AT THE ZOOS.
6Ø LAST WEEKEND WE WENT FOR A RIDE.
65 THE SHIPS HAD RUN AGROUND AGAIN.
7Ø MY MOM AND DAD ARE AWAY AT WORK.
75 WHEN WAS THAT TO HAVE BEEN DONE?
8Ø HE RAN QUITE FAST OVER THE HILL.
```

Alphabetic Practice

WHEN USING A COMPUTER KEYBOARD, GO TO PAGE 27.

This exercise shows you how to correct some simple errors that may be made when entering information on a computer keyboard. (Numeric errors are corrected in the same way.) Remember you are using the typewriter keyboard to simulate a computer keyboard.

The key statement is:

```
1∅ MARY WENT TO VISIT FRIENDS.
```

Enter the following:

```
1∅ MARY WENT TO VISIT FRE
```

You notice immediately that you entered the E and not the I. Move your paper up one full line space. press the **backspace key** once and enter IENDS. and press the **return key**.

```
1∅ MARY WENT TO VISIT FRE
                     IENDS.
```

Examine the following errors and the corresponding corrections:

```
1∅ MARY WENT TO VISIT FREINDS.
                         IENDS.
1∅ MARY WENT VISIT FRIENDS.
             TO VISIT FRIENDS.
1∅ MARY WENT TO VISSIT FRIENDS.
                   VISIT
1∅ MSTY ERNY YO BIDIY GTIRNFD.
   MARY WENT TO VISIT FRIENDS.
```

Correcting Errors on a Typewriter Keyboard

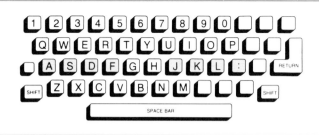

INSTRUCTIONS

Enter each line twice.

Keep your eyes on the copy in the book.

```
1Ø  AID COB END HEM PAP TIE AIR EYE
15  JAM PEN TOT ANT COT FIG JAY TOW
2Ø  CUB FIT LAM ROD URN BID FIX LAP
25  WAR WIG BOB FOE MAN RUB BOG CUT
3Ø  DIE FOX MEN RUT BOX DOE FUR RYE
35  FOAM PAIR SLAP BOWL NIGHT SHAPE
4Ø  BUCK FORM PANE SOAP WHALE FLAKE
45  DISK GIRL LAKE PANT SIGHT CHAIR
5Ø  COAL FIRM MALE FISH SNAKE ELBOW
55  BODY CITY IRIS SIGN TITLE FIELD
6Ø  HEIGHT SLEIGH AIRMAN APT HANDLE
65  TURKEY END LAMENT GOSPEL HANDLE
7Ø  LITERS CHAPEL BIT MANTLE PROFIT
75  ICY ENAMEL SOCIAL ENSIGN SIGNAL
```

Alphabetic Practice

FINGER POSITION

• Place your fingers on the home row keys.

INSTRUCTIONS

Enter each line twice.

Keep your eyes on the copy in the book.

```
1Ø ALL ASH DAD FAD GAG GAS SAD LAD
15 FALL FLAG FLAK GASH SALAD GLASS
2Ø SASH SHAG SAGA GLAD SLASH FLASK
25 ADDS JADE ASKS GAGS FLAGS FLASH
3Ø HALL HASH LASH LASS SHALL JADES
35 EWE EYE TIE IRE TIP ORE TOE PEP
4Ø TOP TOW PIE TOY TWO WOE POT PUP
45 TIER PIER TIRE PIPE TUTOR ERROR
5Ø TOUR PORT TYPE TREE WORRY QUOTE
55 PITY POET RIOT TRIO POPPY POWER
6Ø WIRE QUIP TRUE PURE OTTER ROTOR
65 POOR PORE TRIP PEER HOPES FLAWS
7Ø CALL CALM MALL MASK SCALD SMACK
75 ZOOS FLAX CASH CANS WOMAN BLACK
8Ø MAZE NUMB HAND CAME NAVAL SLACK
```

Alphabetic Practice